NATIVE AMERICAN CULTURES

NATIVE AMERICAN
CEREMONIES AND
CELEBRATIONS

FROM POTLATCHES TO POWWOWS

BY KATE MIKOLEY

Gareth Stevens
PUBLISHING

Please visit our website, www.garethstevens.com. For a free color catalog of all our high-quality books, call toll free 1-800-542-2595 or fax 1-877-542-2596.

Cataloging-in-Publication Data

Names: Mikoley, Kate.
Title: Native American ceremonies and celebrations: from potlatches to powwows / Kate Mikoley.
Description: New York : Gareth Stevens Publishing, 2018. | Series: Native American cultures | Includes index.
Identifiers: ISBN 9781538208885 (pbk.) | ISBN 9781538208908 (library bound) | ISBN 9781538208892 (6 pack)
Subjects: LCSH: Indians of North America–Rites and ceremonies–Juvenile literature. | Indians of North America–Social life and customs–Juvenile literature. | Powwows–Juvenile literature.
Classification: LCC E98.R53 M55 2018 | DDC 970.004'97–dc23

First Edition

Published in 2018 by
Gareth Stevens Publishing
111 East 14th Street, Suite 349
New York, NY 10003

Designer: Sarah Liddell
Editor: Therese Shea

Photo credits: Cover, p. 1 (main image) Golden Shrimp/Shutterstock.com; cover, pp. 1 (photograph), 6 US National Archives bot/Wikimedia Commons; cover, p. 1 (rattle) Uyvsdi/Wikimedia Commons; p. 5 Ævar Arnfjörð Bjarmason/Wikimedia Commons; p. 7 SreeBot/Wikimedia Commons; p. 9 Gregory Johnston/Shutterstock.com; p. 10 Audrey Snider-Bell/Shutterstock.com; p. 11 Culture Club/Contributor/ Hulton Archive/Getty Images; p. 12 Nativestock.com/Marilyn Angel Wynn/Nativestock/Getty Images; p. 13 Buyenlarge/Contributor/Archive Photos/Getty Images; p. 14 Kaitlyn153/Wikimedia Commons; p. 15 photo courtesy of Library of Congress; p. 17 Nesnad/Wikimedia Commons; p. 19 Nathan Benn/Contributor/Corbis Historical/Getty Images; p. 20 Geoffrey Clements/Contributor/Corbis Historical/Getty Images; p. 21 ullstein bild/Contributor/ullstein bild/Getty Images; p. 22 Ralph Crane/ Contributor/The LIFE Picture Collection/Getty Images; p. 23 Patrick Endres/Design Pics/First Light/ Getty Images; p. 25 Slowking4/Wikimedia Commons; p. 26 M. Unal Ozmen/Shutterstock.com; p. 27 Yann/Wikimedia Commons; p. 28 Magnus Manske/Wikimedia Commons; p. 29 Alina R/ Shutterstock.com.

Printed in the United States of America

CPSIA compliance information: Batch #CW18GS: For further information contact Gareth Stevens, New York, New York at 1-800-542-2595.

CONTENTS

Words in the glossary appear in **bold** type the first time they are used in the text.

THE FIRST AMERICANS

The first people to live in a place are called indigenous (ihn-DIH-juh-nuhs) people. Native Americans are the indigenous peoples of the United States. They lived in the area long before it was called the United States and thousands of years before Europeans even arrived.

The many **cultures** of Native Americans are full of one-of-a-kind **traditions**. Important events are often marked by **ceremonies**. These ceremonies are deeply based in religion, or ways of honoring a god or gods, as well as respect for nature and Native Americans' **ancestors**.

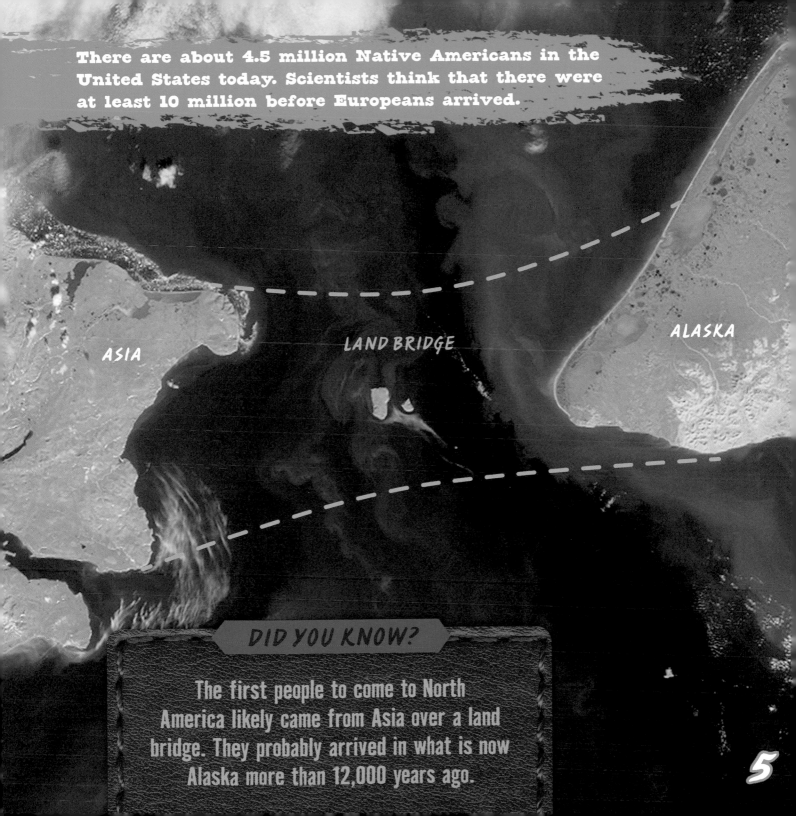

There are about 4.5 million Native Americans in the United States today. Scientists think that there were at least 10 million before Europeans arrived.

ASIA

LAND BRIDGE

ALASKA

DID YOU KNOW?

The first people to come to North America likely came from Asia over a land bridge. They probably arrived in what is now Alaska more than 12,000 years ago.

Perhaps the most well-known Native American **celebration** is the powwow. This is an event in which people, often from several Native American nations, come together to dance, sing, and honor the traditions of the past.

Europeans witnessed Algonquian-speaking Northeast Indians gathering for a **curing** ceremony in the 1800s. They called it a "powwow," after the Algonquian word *pau-wau* or *pauau*, which was a meeting of **spiritual** leaders. Soon, any Native American dancing ceremony was called a "powwow."

TURTLE SHELL RATTLES WORN BY DANCERS

Modern powwows are different from the ceremonies of the early Native Americans, but they're rooted in many of the same traditions.

DID YOU KNOW?

Gatherings similar to powwows have existed in most Native American communities since long before Europeans came to North America.

A CHANGING EVENT

In the 19th and 20th centuries, the US government tried to stop Native Americans from practicing many of their traditions. However, the powwow survived. Some of its features have changed, but its meaning and importance remains.

Powwows today can last anywhere from 1 to 4 days. Dancers, singers, and artists from hundreds of miles away attend these community gatherings. Many powwows are open to the public. Some even offer prize money for dance and music events. People travel all over the country to **compete** at powwows!

8

The songs and dances at modern powwows often come from the traditions of the early **Plains** peoples.

THE SNAKE DANCE

The Hopi are a group of Native Americans who live mostly in Arizona today. Arizona is often hot and dry, so certain Hopi ceremonies ask gods and spirits for rain.

Part of one Hopi ceremony, the Snake Dance, was once open for the public to see. During the 16-day event, the Hopi gathered snakes. Then, some people danced with the snakes in their mouth. Finally, the snakes were let go in all directions to carry prayers for rain to the gods.

RATTLESNAKE

DID YOU KNOW?

Rattlesnakes were sometimes chosen for the Hopi's Snake Dance.

The taking of illegal photos is partly why the public can no longer attend the Hopi ceremony.

11

THE SUN DANCE

Different forms of the religious ceremony called the Sun Dance exist throughout Native American cultures. It served different purposes for different peoples. For most, it was a way to connect with ancestors, nature, and each other.

During the Sun Dance of the Plains peoples, Native Americans gathered for several days and danced with few breaks. They didn't eat food or drink water throughout this time. Though they grew weak, they believed they gathered great spiritual power.

SUN DANCE LODGE

Some Native American communities centered the Sun Dance around a tall pole. This pole was thought to be a connection to a god or gods.

13

THE POTLATCH

A potlatch was a kind of party put on mostly by Native Americans who lived in the Pacific Northwest. People played music, made speeches, and danced.

Traditionally, potlatches were given in honor of marriages, births, and deaths. However, the reason for the event didn't matter. The potlatch was a way for someone to show how important they were in their community. The bigger the potlatch, the more important the **host**. Potlatches were a way for **rivals** to try to outdo each other!

SPEAKER FIGURE

DID YOU KNOW?

People who had been shamed in public could throw a potlatch to regain good standing in the community.

Potlatches were attended by many people in a community. Guests were provided with two large meals each day.

HAIDA POTLATCH

PREPARING FOR THE PARTY

The people who attended a potlatch didn't bring gifts to their host. They were given gifts! Hosts collected wealth so that they could give it away. By accepting gifts, guests were accepting the host's importance in their community. The people with the highest position in the community would receive the most, but everyone received something. Goods included money, food, and clothing.

Potlatches could last for several days. A chief's potlatch was planned for many years. Some groups still practice the potlatch today.

DID YOU KNOW?

In the 1880s, Tsimshian chief Ligeex hosted a potlatch in Canada, though the government had banned them. He hid the goods that were to be given away!

The word "potlatch" is from the Nuu-chah-nulth word *p'alshit*, which means "to give." The Nuu-chah-nulth people live on the west coast of Vancouver Island in Canada.

17

THE FALSE FACE SOCIETY

Throughout history, many have used ceremonies to try to heal sick people. Medicine societies are Native American groups formed to cure illness.

The most famous of the medicine societies was the False Face Society of the Haudenosaunee (sometimes called Iroquois), who were largely located in and around New York State. Members carved, or cut, wooden masks from living trees. When a person was sick, members of the society held a special ceremony. They wore the masks while dancing for the sick person to drive away the illness.

DID YOU KNOW?

A healed person became a member of the False Face Society of the Haudenosaunee (hoh-dee-nuh-SHOH-nee).

The Haudenosaunee are against displaying their sacred masks in pictures. A Haudenosaunee man is shown here in traditional dress in front of a longhouse.

THE BLESSINGWAY

A main healing ceremony in Navajo communities is a **chant** called the Blessingway, or the "song of songs." However, the Blessingway isn't meant to cure sickness. Instead, it's used to bring blessings and prevent bad luck.

The Blessingway generally lasts two nights, but it's sometimes part of longer ceremonies. Its songs speak of the first peoples and how they overcame evil. Sometimes the singer, often a male, uses a rattle during the Blessingway. Navajo also create sand paintings, or dry paintings, as part of the ceremony.

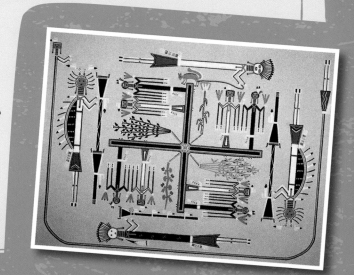

NAVAJO SAND PAINTING

NAVAJO MAN PAINTING
HEALING SYMBOLS

The Navajo make up the second-largest group of
Native Americans in the United States. They live
mostly in New Mexico, Arizona, and Utah.

THE INUPIAT BLANKET TOSS

The Inupiat are a native people of northern Alaska. They mark the end of whale-hunting season in June with a celebration of thanks called Nalukataq. It includes prayers, songs, dancing, stories, and a blanket toss.

For the blanket toss, men and women gather in a circle and hold the ends of a large blanket made of sealskin. Then, they take turns bouncing on it and trying to land on their feet. Some do flips! Jumpers lose their turn if they lose their balance.

DID YOU KNOW?

The blanket toss may have begun as a way for hunters to spot animals from far away!

The person on the blanket often throws gifts into the crowd. Usually, ship captains go first.

THE GREEN CORN CEREMONY

Many cultures around the world have ceremonies to celebrate the first harvest, or crop, of the year. The Green Corn Ceremony is one such celebration in many Native American communities, such as the Choctaw, who were indigenous to the Southeast.

Ceremonies differ depending on the group, but they often feature prayers, dancing, and games. Thanks are given to the gods for the rain, sun, corn, and other crops. Fasting, or not eating for a period of time, is often part of the ceremony, too.

DID YOU KNOW?

Some Choctaw were forced to move to Oklahoma. They still practice the Green Corn Ceremony there.

This image shows the Sioux Green Corn Ceremony in 1860. The celebration continues to be important in many native communities.

25

THE FIRST LAUGH CEREMONY

From a baby's first steps to their first words, people often celebrate the firsts in a child's life. In the Navajo community, a baby's first laugh is a very important event. Some believe the laugh means the baby has left the spiritual world and is now fully human. A feast is given to honor the occasion, often within 4 days of the laugh.

The baby is considered the host of the celebration. However, the person who made the baby laugh is often in charge of preparing for it.

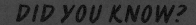

DID YOU KNOW?

The person putting on the ceremony helps the baby give guests salt, a sign of goodness. It's meant to be the first of many acts of kindness in the baby's life.

In the Navajo tradition, children belong to the world of the Holy People. Laughter is a sign they're ready to live with their earthly family.

CONTINUING CULTURES

Many Native American peoples were forced to leave their homes as settlers spread across North America. Native Americans were told to stop practicing ceremonies and to accept the ways of white culture.

Luckily, some Native Americans held fast to their traditions, even practicing them in secret. That's why ceremonies still survive today. One of the best ways to learn more about an indigenous culture is to attend an event open to the public. It's a perfect way to show support and respect for Native American cultures.

Today, people of all ages still take part in many
important Native American celebrations.

GLOSSARY

ancestor: a person in past times who is in someone's family

celebration: a time to show happiness for an event through activities such as eating or playing music

ceremony: an event to honor or celebrate something

chant: a kind of singing using a small number of musical notes repeated many times

compete: to try to get or win something that someone else is also trying to win

culture: the beliefs and ways of life of a group of people

cure: to make someone healthy again

host: a person who takes care of guests

medicine: something used in treating illness or easing pain

rival: a person who tries to be more successful than another

spiritual: of or having to do with a person's spirit and beliefs

tradition: a way of thinking or doing something that has been done by a people or a group for a long time

FOR MORE INFORMATION

BOOKS

Ciovacco, Justine. *Discovering Native North American Cultures.* New York, NY: Britannica Educational Publishing, 2015.

Weil, Ann, and Charlotte Guillain. *American Indian Cultures.* Chicago, IL: Heinemann Library, 2013.

WEBSITES

Native American Facts for Kids
www.native-languages.org/kids.htm
Find out more about Native American peoples here.

The Powwow
nativeamericans.mrdonn.org/powwow.html
Learn about the dances and traditions of a powwow.

INDEX